Dance!

**No matter what kind of
dance you like to do,
this book is for you.**

by Apryl Lundsten
illustrated by Helen Dardik

⭐ American Girl®

Published by American Girl Publishing, Inc.

Questions or comments? Call 1-800-845-0005,
visit our Web site at **americangirl.com**,
or write to Customer Service, American Girl, 8400 Fairway Place,
Middleton, WI 53562-0497.

Printed in China

08 09 10 11 12 13 LEO 10 9 8 7 6 5 4 3 2 1

All American Girl marks are trademarks of American Girl, LLC.

Editorial Development: Carrie Anton

Art Direction & Design: Chris Lorette David

Production: Mindy Rappe, Jeannette Bailey, Judith Lary,
Gretchen Krause

Illustrations: Helen Dardik

Photography: Radlund Studios

Special thanks to DeAnne Boegli, Beth Fried, Joya Powell,
Athletic Garage Dance Studio, Blackbird Studio, Destiny Arts
Center, and the Russian Ballet Company of Indiana.

Dear Reader,

People can usually pick a dancer out of a crowd. She's the one with the **confident posture,** proud walk, and air of self-respect. Dancing can make a difference in your everyday life. It can boost your self-confidence, help you learn to **love your body,** and encourage you to try new things—on and off the dance floor.

So whether you **dance in your room** to your favorite tunes or have dreams of being a **ballerina onstage,** this book will inspire you to find the dancer within you.

You'll learn what to do to **get your feet moving** and what it's like to dance in class. Plus, you'll hear from girls—just like you—who describe why they love to dance.

So turn the page to get your toes tapping!

Your friends at American Girl

Find Your Groove

Discover the dancer within you, because dancing . . .

1. can make you feel good about yourself.

2. allows you to express yourself.

3. can shift your mood and turn a bad day into a great one!

4. is good for your body—and mind.

5. is fun!

Loosen Up

Warm up your muscles—and mind—to get ready to move.

Smiley Face Exercise

Try this simple exercise to see how a smile can help you let loose:

Stand in front of a mirror.
Now smile.
Then frown.
Then smile again really big.
Then frown really big.
Keep doing it faster and faster.
You'll probably end up laughing and notice a change in how you feel.

Each time you do this, try to get your whole body involved—not just your mouth. When you smile, try to stand up straighter. And when you frown, let your back go loose. Find fun ways to transfer these movements into your arms, hands, legs, and feet.

Frown.

Now
smile!

Let Loose

Stand in front of a mirror.

Let your arms hang down by your sides.

Shake your head from side to side.

Shimmy your shoulders.

Wiggle your hips.

Do all of this at once, getting your body as loose as possible.

Stretch Tall

Reach your arms high up into the air, reaching for the ceiling.
Now bend down and reach for your toes, trying to stretch to the ground.
Do this five times.

V-Leg Stretch

Sit down with your legs in a "V" shape.
Stretch your body over your right leg.
Hold for 30 seconds to really feel the stretch.
Then stretch your body over your left leg.
Hold for 30 seconds.
Now stretch in the center,
again holding for 30 seconds.

Side Stretch

Stand tall with your right arm above
your head.
Keep your legs shoulder-width apart.
Bend at the waist over your left side.
Hold for 30 seconds.
Come back to the center.
Raise your left arm and bend at the
waist over your right side.
Hold for 30 seconds.
Come back to the center.
Do this stretch twice on each side.

On Your Feet

What you need to start moving

Comfy Clothes
Throw on some sweats and a T-shirt or shorts and a tank top.

Plenty of Room
Find space in your house or clear some space in your bedroom. Have Mom or Dad help if you need to move a chair or desk.

Music
Turn on the radio or put on a CD. Even if you don't have music on hand, you can hum or sing a song.

An Open Mind
Don't think about how you look when you dance. And if you do look silly, laugh about it! Remember, the most important thing about dancing is that it makes you feel good!

Now all that's left is to get moving. So . . . jump up and down! Shake your shoulders! Wave your hands in the air! See? That's all it takes. Look at you— you're a dancer!

Still not feeling the beat? Get inspired!

Five songs to make you want to move

1. "YMCA" by The Village People
2. "Got to Be Real" by Cheryl Lynn
3. "September" by Earth, Wind and Fire
4. "Groove Is in the Heart" by Dee-Lite
5. "Dancing Queen" by ABBA

Must-See Dance Movies

Annie
High School Musical
Singin' in the Rain
White Christmas
The Wizard of Oz

I started dancing when I was 2. My mom is also a dancer, so she really inspired me. I love the way dancing lets me express how I'm feeling.
Soleil, age 9

Set the Steps

Create choreography by combining cool moves.

Choreography is the art of creating dance steps. A **choreographer** is the person who creates those steps.

You can make dance moves out of any movement or familiar object, such as a moving car or a growing flower; an animal such as a cat or dog; or a person such as your little sister or grandpa.

The idea is to **bring the object to life** through your movements. To do this, start by mimicking or interpreting the object. Pretend you are a rose in a garden on a warm afternoon. What does that feel like? What movements can you use to express being a petal, gently touched by the sun and soft breeze?

You might feel silly or awkward doing these exercises at first, but they'll help you become a better dancer in the end.

Tiger Crawl

Pretend you're a tiger in the jungle.
Get down on all fours.
Crawl as if you're moving through tall grass.
Swipe at the grass with your claws.
Give a fierce look.
Make the movements slow, and then fast.

Basketball Boogie
Dribble an imaginary basketball.
Skip, run, dance across the imaginary court.
Shoot the ball at the hoop.
Keep doing this, making your movements
looser and more exaggerated each time.

Now you be the choreographer.
Pretend you're dancing on the moon. What does that look like? Remember, there's not much gravity on the moon. How do you keep your feet on the ground? How will your arms move? Find music that sounds *out of this world,* and match up your movements to the beat.

Game Time

Grab some friends and get in step with these fun dance games!

Last Girl Dancing
Have a dance contest to see who can dance the longest without stopping.

Get Down
Make cards with different dances written on each. Place the cards in a bowl, hat, or bag and have each person choose one before each song. The game can be played so that either the girl who chooses the card has to dance or the whole group can do the chosen dance together.

Soundtracks
Put on one of your favorite movie soundtracks, such as *Shrek* or *The Princess Diaries*, and dance as characters from the movies would.

Act It Out
Make up dance steps that go along with the lyrics of a song to tell the story. For example, if a singer cries out "Call me," pretend you're talking on the phone. The more dramatic you are, the better.

Video Moves
For cool dance-step ideas, take a close look at dancers on music videos. Try out the steps with your guests.

My little sister got me excited about dancing. She was really into it, and I used to just watch. But it looked like so much fun that I wanted to get up and do it, too! Now we dance together whenever we can.
Lenise, age 9

Bookworm to Ballerina

Stereotype. That's how I've always felt—like a stereotype. See, I'm considered "the smart girl." You know, the bookworm. The one who answers questions in class. The girl who's picked last in gym because she's uncoordinated at sports with a ball.

But in my heart I am more than just brainy—I'm also a dancer! I've been taking ballet since I was little. It makes me feel as if I have wings and can soar, and it has helped me understand my body. With each turn and leap, I've learned my strengths and weaknesses. I know I can push myself and be physical—even if it's not in a traditional physical education way.

Ballet technique is very precise, but I love it because I can make each dance my own by letting my emotions shine through. Whatever I'm feeling—whether it's happiness, sadness, or stress—I put it into my dancing and reveal my heart and soul. When I dance, everything else seems to melt away, leaving just my love and passion for ballet.

This past year, my dream to dance *en pointe* came true after I received my first pair of pointe shoes. When I first saw myself in the mirror in these shoes, the stereotypes that others had used to define me began to fade away. I was no longer the clumsy bookworm but a strong, graceful, and beautiful dancer. Thanks to ballet —and my brains—dance has helped me see and love myself for who I really am. And I know that's more important than what anyone else thinks of me.

Allison, age 12

Class Act

Making the grade in dance class and onstage

Dos & Don'ts of Dancewear

Clothes to wear to class

Dancewear Dos

- **Do** ask your teacher what's appropriate to wear to class. Some studios have dress codes.
- **Do** keep it simple with a basic leotard and tights.
- **Do** wear pants that are made with stretchy fabrics, such as Lycra. You'll be able to bend and stretch more easily.
- **Do** wear clothes that are made with cotton. Cotton breathes and will keep you cool when you dance.
- **Do** have your hair tied back in a ponytail or a bun.
- **Do** clip long bangs back with a barrette—or hold them back with one of the headband ideas in the back of the book.
- **Do** wear the right shoes for the type of dance class you're taking.

Dancewear Don'ts

- **Don't** wear jeans. Jeans aren't stretchy enough.
- **Don't** wear pants that are too long—they'll drag on the floor and trip you up.
- **Don't** wear dangling jewelry. Take off big earrings or long necklaces.
- **Don't** wear anything that's too baggy. Baggy clothes can make it hard to move.
- **Don't** wear shoes that are the wrong size. You can't two-step if you're swimming in your shoes or they're pinching your toes.

Love Your Look . . . Even in a Leotard

Here are some ways to love your look no matter what.

• Express yourself with dancewear in fun colors or
  styles. Wear a brightly colored, sparkly, or boldly
  patterned leotard.

• Add a ballet skirt over your leotard. You can find
  skirts at your local dancewear store, or create your
  own! Wrap Mom's scarf around your waist to create a
  one-of-a-kind sarong.

• Layer your look by adding a long tank over the top of
  your leotard or a fitted long-sleeved tee under your
  leotard.

• Cover your shoulders with a shrug (a short sweater)—
  this is the classic ballerina look. Or cover your legs
  with leg warmers.

• Wear leggings or yoga pants over your leotard.

Again, be sure to ask your teacher what's appropriate
to wear to class. Some ballet teachers don't allow
students to wear anything over their leotards because
they need to see how your knees, elbows, legs,
and arms move. But if your studio allows it, express
yourself with fun dancewear.

Lesson One

What to expect at your first class

Dancers

Most classes will have about ten other dancers just like you, who are also taking lessons for the first time.

Follow the Leader

Your teacher will demonstrate in front of the class first. Then you'll try. Often the teacher will come around the room and correct you. Don't worry—she isn't telling you you're doing a bad job. She's just helping you have the proper technique and stay safe.

Early Bird

Come to class a few minutes early to stretch on your own. Arriving early will also give you time to hang out and chat with your dance friends before class begins.

My first class was really fun—I made a lot of friends . . . even with the teacher! I would say that what I love most about dancing is the music, the dancing, and my friends.

Adamma, age 9

Smooth Moves

Focus on the footwork first. Then add the arms once you feel comfortable with the steps.

Be Patient

Learning new moves can be hard, but just keep trying and soon you'll get it. Remember that you're doing something new! It often takes several classes—and lots of practice—to learn the choreography.

Friendly Advice

If you're struggling with the steps, you might make a friend by asking a classmate how to do a move you don't understand. Asking for help is a great icebreaker—and you just might learn that tricky spin!

Team Player

Dancing is a team sport, like basketball, which takes cooperation and sportsmanship. Your classmates are your teammates, and you have to work together. Plus, like basketball players, dancers are athletes. You'll be putting as much work into class as any other athlete does at her sport's practice.

The No-Clique Zone

When you come to dance class, leave the cliques at the door. Even if you have a tight group of friends at school, branch out in dance class. You're likely going to be taking dance classes with the same kids for a while, so you need to remain respectful and supportive of one another. Class is a great opportunity to make new friends—and eventually your classmates may even feel like a second family.

Climbing the Dance Ladder

If you're going to start taking classes at your best friend's studio, don't expect to be in the same class. If she's been taking classes for a while, she's going to be ahead of you. It doesn't matter if you're the same age—you need to work your way up.

Listen and Learn

Each student needs to listen carefully to ALL corrections. The teacher might pick one student to be the example, but chances are, the whole class probably has the same issue.

Shhh . . .

Don't talk in class. It can be really distracting. Everyone needs to be able to hear the teacher—including you! Instead, socialize before and after class.

Teacher Talk

Need help? Here's how to get it!

Your **teacher** can be a great role model. She also can be a friend and be there to help you. If you're **struggling with a routine** during class, your teacher will probably notice and try to help you. If she doesn't, raise your hand and ask your question or have her demonstrate the step again. Chances are, other students are probably having the same concerns as you are, so **your question will be helping the whole class**.

If you still don't understand something, just **try your best and keep going**, concentrating as much as you can. Then stay after class to ask any questions. For example, ask, "Do you have any extra hints for me? Or do you have some notes I can take home to practice with? (Hint: bring your own notebook to write down the steps.) Having your teacher write down a difficult combination for you to practice at home is a great way to learn. And **practicing at home can help you improve quickly.**

Once you've talked to your teacher, she'll know to watch you next time in class and can give you extra help when you need it.

I love being taught by a teacher because I really learn a lot. I know that if I can learn steps or routines that I think are hard, I can do other things that might seem hard, too.

Larissa, age 11

Practice Makes Better

What you do out of class can make you better in class.

Remove Distractions
That means no TV, no phone, no IMing—and try to make sure your little brother leaves you alone, too!

Get the Music
Ask your instructor for a copy of the music. In situations where you can't dance, such as in the car, listen to the music and go over the moves in your mind.

Partner Up
Practice with a friend. Her feedback could help you improve, and you'll get used to dancing in front of an audience.

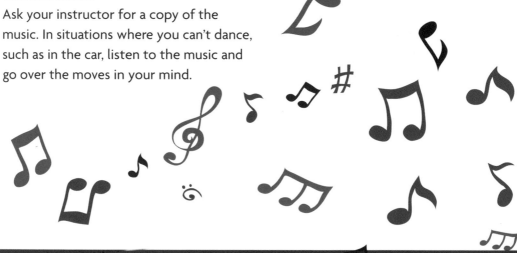

Set Realistic Goals

Create a dance journal and put your goals on paper. When you write things down, you may become more committed to making them happen.

Think about your dance goals. Check the things you'd like to accomplish:

- ☐ Become more comfortable dancing in public
- ☐ Learn how to do a difficult move, such as a pirouette
- ☐ Try out for a musical
- ☐ Make new friends
- ☐ Get more exercise
- ☐ Become a better dancer
- ☐ Feel more confident at the school dance
- ☐ Create a dance group
- ☐ Enter a dance competition

Tryouts

Questions and answers to help you ace your audition

Many performances, such as school musicals and talent shows, require some kind of tryout or audition. A *tryout* is a sample performance that allows a dancer to show how well she can dance. This helps the dance instructor or show director figure out what role is the best fit for the dancer's talents and skills.

Q: My first audition is coming up and I'm really nervous. What should I do?

A: First, remember that everyone else is just as nervous as you are. To help you stay calm before you go onstage, try a breathing exercise.

Start by taking a deep breath and holding it for one count. Then let it go. Repeat this five times to calm yourself down. Try holding your breath a little longer each time.

Q: How can I make sure my body is prepared for tryouts?

A: Eat. Make sure you've eaten something before you audition. Dancing on an empty stomach can zap you of much-needed energy. A small healthy snack such as low-fat yogurt, string cheese, or fruit is good for energy.

Drink. Bring a bottle of water with you to tryouts and make sure you drink plenty of it. Your muscles need to be well hydrated.

Rest. Get plenty of sleep the night before tryouts. Being well rested will help you focus.

Stretch. Make sure your muscles are warmed up.

Q: How can I stay positive during auditions?

A: Smile. Believe it or not, just the simple act of smiling can make you feel happy. Plus, everyone watching will notice your smile and recognize how much you love dancing.

Think Positive Thoughts. See yourself doing a great job at your audition, and it will happen!

Just Another Dance. Don't think of it as an audition but as just another dance. You dance because you enjoy it, so just get out there and have fun—because that's what is most important.

Q: Should I talk to the other dancers trying out? Or should I just keep to myself?

A: Being focused is a good thing, but being lost in your own world isn't. Everyone is in the same boat, and each dancer could use some encouragement. Compliment the other dancers by saying "Good job." Being friendly will lift everyone's spirits. Plus, you might make a new friend.

Q: What happens if I don't get picked?

A: Not making the cut can be disappointing—but it's not the end of the world. Just pick yourself up and try out for the next opportunity. Remember, trying out for a show is a really big deal. You should be proud each time you give it a shot, whether you get a part or not. Be sure to celebrate your audition in some way. Maybe treat yourself to something special—rent a movie you've been wanting to see, or spend time with your best friend. You can also celebrate your auditions by keeping mementos in a memory box or photo album as a record of your accomplishments.

Q: I got a part in our school's musical, but it's not the one I wanted. What should I do?

A: First of all, congratulations! You got a part. So it's not the one you wanted—that's O.K. Even the smallest part allows you to grow, learn, and, most importantly, *dance*. And that's what it's all about! Take your role as seriously as if you got the lead. Work hard at rehearsals and even practice at home—that way you can give the best possible performance.

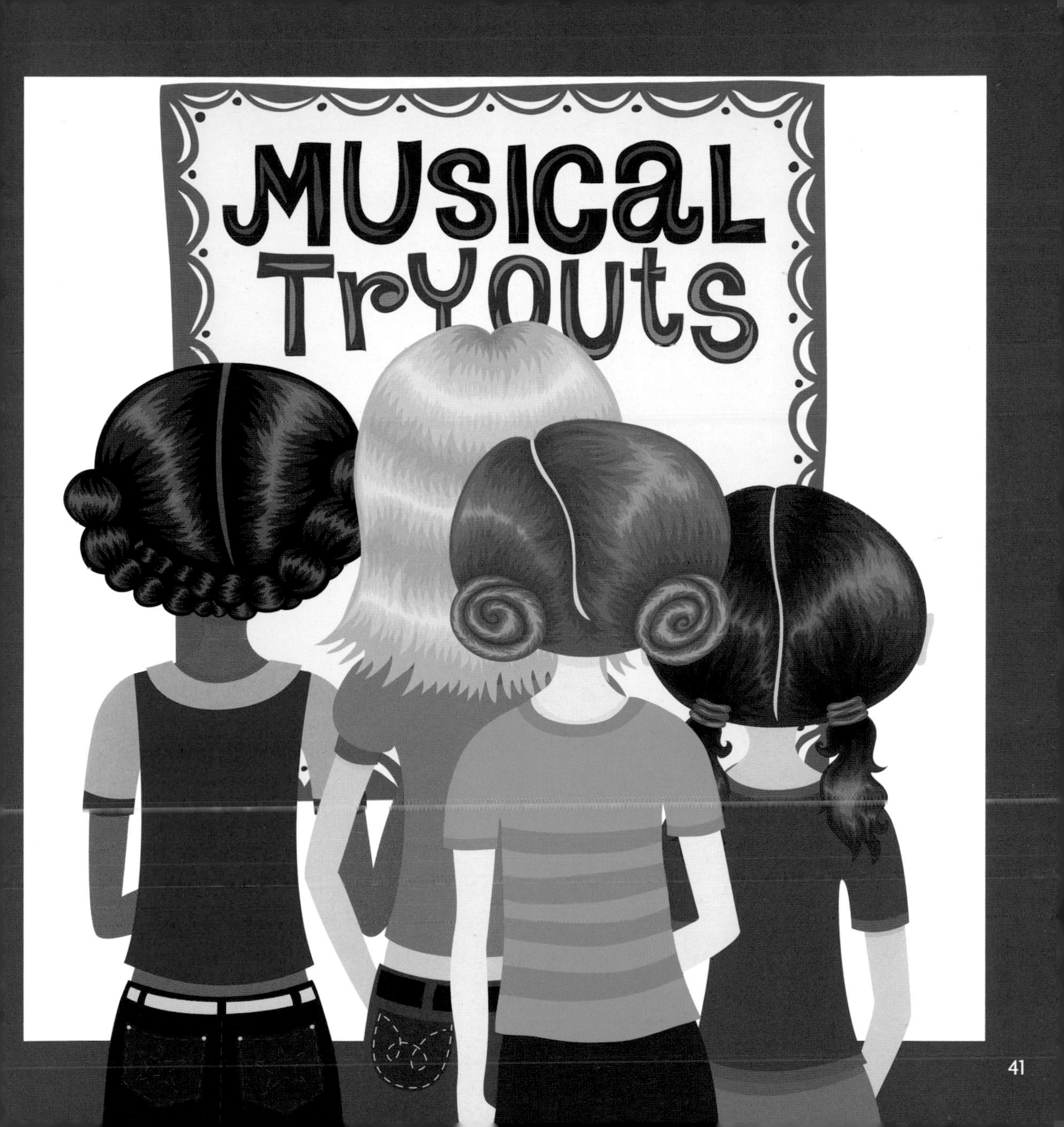
MUSICAL
TRYOUTS

Showtime

Performance tips for when the curtain goes up

Stretch

It's important to stretch before a performance. Not only will it warm up your body, but stretching can help you chill out.

Just Excited, Not Scared

When you get butterflies in your stomach, remind yourself that your body is just giving you the extra energy you need for an awesome performance.

Counting—5, 6, 7, 8

Make sure not to move your lips while you count. Just count silently to yourself.

Bring Your Fan Club

Invite your family and maybe a friend or two to your performance. That way you'll have a few people in the audience to cheer you on. Knowing that you're dancing for people who support you and love you can help take your jitters away.

Catch Up

If you get lost during the routine, follow the person in front of you to get back on track.

Go For It

Think some of those moves are going to make you look silly? Well, if you hold back and don't give it your all, you're going to look as if you don't know what you're doing—and that can really make you look silly!

Don't Hog the Spotlight

Your whole dance team is onstage. Remember, the goal is for people to look at the team, not just at you.

Say "Cheese!" Make sure you look out over the audience and SMILE!

Mis-Steps

Tips for dealing with two left feet

If you do mess up, keep going. Most of the time only YOU will know you made a mistake.

If you fall, pick yourself up and get back into the routine. The audience will admire you for not letting a mistake bother you.

Don't keep thinking about the fact that you just tripped. In the same way that you have to move on with the steps, **move on with your thoughts.**

Sometimes it's tricky enough just remembering the steps you have to do, let alone the steps that follow. But try not to let it trip you up. If you dance in a group and can't remember a move, **take a look around to see what others are**

doing. If you're dancing solo when you freeze, take a deep breath and jump back in when you're ready.

Smile, smile, smile. Don't let the mistake show on your face. If your feet wobble but your face stays the same, you won't reveal that you messed up. And people will be less likely to notice.

If you have a costume problem, such as dropping a prop or losing your hat, **keep dancing as if nothing happened.** Even if an item is in the way, just step over it or kick it out of the way. Pick it up later when you clear the stage. Don't let it be a distraction through the whole routine.

Don't dwell on your mistakes later. It's not necessary to tell everyone that you messed up. If someone brings it up, laugh it off—don't deny it, but don't make a big deal about it either.

And remember . . . there's always the next performance.

Sometimes I mess up, but my dance teachers say to keep going. If you just stop and stand there, people will notice. But if you move on and keep going, the audience won't even know you made a mistake.

Teryn, age 12

Steps to Recovery

A true story

I've been dancing all my life. Ever since I can remember, I've been taking classes and performing in recitals. I love being onstage and performing for people. I've taken tap, swing, ballet, and lyrical—they're all fun! But my favorite styles are jazz and hip-hop. I've always felt as if dancing is a gift I need to share with the world. But I never realized how important dancing was to me until recently, when I got sick.

I started having terrible stomach pains, and the doctors didn't know what was wrong with me. They did exploratory surgery and took my appendix out. When I went home, I was in a lot of pain and had to take pain medicine, which made me really groggy. Still, with a competition coming up in only two weeks, all I could think about was dancing.

The doctors didn't think I'd be able to compete. But I was determined. I rested for a week, staying in bed the whole time and going through the routine over and over in my head. By the second week I knew I couldn't stay in bed anymore. I just had to dance! My parents checked with the doctor, and because I was healing so well, I was given the O.K. to head back to the studio—so long as I took it slow. At first, I just walked through the routine; that was all I could do. But each day it got a little better

and I could dance a little more. The more
I danced, the more the pain went away, and
I could feel myself getting well. The doctors
were amazed at how fast I recovered.

When competition day came around, I got
onstage and danced my heart out. I was just
so happy to be able to dance. Whether my
team placed or not didn't matter to me.
Without dance I know it would have taken a
lot longer for me to heal. Dancing helped me
forget the pain and gave me the strength I
needed to get well. Dancing is my gift to me.
Now I know I can get through anything!
Alyssa, age 10

Steppin' Out

Tips for dancing with other people

Look at Me

Dance in public without fear

Besides performances on a stage, there are other places where you might dance in front of people:

Your aunt's wedding

The school dance

A friend's party

The secret to dancing is that **there is no secret.** People simply listen to music and make up the moves as they go. It's not as if you have to fake it. All you need to do is stand up.

Just as you practice dancing to learn new steps, you can practice feeling more comfortable dancing in front of others. **Dance in front of your family.** Even ask Mom or Dad to show you some moves. **Dance with your friends.** The more you dance around others, the less your nerves will get the better of you.

Dancing is about having a good time. So let loose and be happy!

I make dancing my own by the way I move. Because I make up steps that express who I am, I'm not afraid to dance in front of people.
Jayla, age 13

51

School Dance

Questions and answers about dancing with classmates

Does going to a school dance give you the jitters? Don't worry—we've got your back—and feet!

Q: What should I wear to a school dance?

A: What you wear depends on what kind of dance it is. Are you going to a winter formal, or a theme dance, such as a 1970s disco? Formal dances require dressier attire. Theme dances are often like costume parties. But for most dances, you can wear what you'd normally wear to school. You want to be comfortable.

Q. I'm really nervous about dancing in front of kids at my school. What should I do?

A: It's perfectly O.K. just to watch for a while. Seeing other people on the dance floor will probably make you feel more comfortable about getting out there. Once you're ready, grab your friends and dance together. Make each other laugh. There's strength in numbers.

Q: I've been taking dance classes. Can I show off some of my moves?

A: Absolutely. Just keep the music in mind. Pop music probably isn't the best for ballet, but you can take some of the steps you've learned and adapt them to whatever song is playing.

Q: My friends and I have been practicing a dance routine. Can we practice it here?

A: A school dance can be a great place to try out your dance routine. You can even teach other kids how to do it.

Q. Do I need a date to go to a school dance?

A. Absolutely not. You can go with your best bud or meet up with a group of your friends when you get there.

Q. What if a boy asks me to slow dance?

A. If you want to dance, say yes! But if the thought of slow dancing gives you butterflies, make some jokes about it. The boy is probably feeling just as nervous as you are—and will likely appreciate your sense of humor. One good thing is that slow dancing is easier than fast dancing. To do it, face your partner. He'll put his right hand on your left hip, while his left hand will gently hold your right hand. Your left hand should be on his shoulder. Then you'll start moving, usually in a circular direction.

If you don't want to slow dance—or dance any dance, for that matter—with a boy, you can say, "No thanks, I'm tired." But if you do that, you shouldn't accept another boy's invitation two seconds later.

Q: What if nobody asks me to dance at all?

A: No biggie. Grab your gal pals and get moving!

It Takes Two

A true story

I never thought I'd be a dancer. Dancing just wasn't something I was into—especially not ballroom dancing. BORING! But when our school started a mandatory ten-week dance course, I had no choice but to take it.

The first day of class was nerve-wracking. Aside from the fact that I didn't know a thing about ballroom dancing and was worried about what the teacher would be like, this kind of dance requires a partner, which means dancing with a boy. I didn't want to at first—touching a boy sounded pretty awful. But our teacher had us hold hands to get used to it. Soon it was no big deal.

We learned how to do the salsa, the rumba, and the tango. Tango is my favorite, because I love the music and the way the dance is a mix of emotion and attitude. After a few weeks of class, our teacher picked the three best couples to compete in the city-wide competition. My partner and I were chosen to dance the rumba. We practiced every day, and when we weren't practicing at school, we got together and practiced at each other's houses. Before this, I never would have thought I could stick to such a strict practice schedule, but it was actually fun. The hard work paid off; we placed in the semifinals at competition.

Ballroom dancing has prepared me for both dancing in public and dancing with boys. Usually at parties I just sat and watched everyone else dance. Not anymore. When my friends and I get together now, we usually dance. I recently had a party and invited all my friends from dance class. At one point we played one of our competition songs, and everyone got up and started dancing. That never would have happened before.

Next year I'm going to middle school, which means I can go to school dances. Before I was part of dance class, the thought of school dances made me nervous. I don't think I would've gone. But now I can't wait! Dancing has helped me in so many areas of my life. I'm much more interested in school, and my grades have even gone up! I'm definitely planning to keep dancing and keep competing when I can. Now I know—I *AM* a dancer.

Damaris, age 12

Heaps of Headbands

Jazz up your 'do and keep your hair out of your face.

Leg-Up Headband

You'll need:
- a pair of leggings you no longer wear
- scissors

Instructions:

1. Ask Mom or Dad if it's O.K. to recycle an old pair of leggings.
2.  With help from an adult, cut a 3-inch strip at the widest part of the leg—or the part that will fit around your head best.
3. To wear, pull the legging strip over your head and down around your neck. Slide the strip up so that it's just past your hairline. Leave bangs in or out. Finish with sparkly hair clips or bobby pins, or leave it plain for a sporty look.

Chain-Tied Headband

You'll need:

• Small hair elastics (number depends on head size)

Instructions:

1. Take one small hair elastic and place it over a second hair elastic so that It forms a cross. Take the left side of the first elastic over the second elastic and through its own right side. Pull to make a knot. Repeat this with as many elastics as you need to reach around your head with a little bit of stretch.

2. To close the chain, fold it in half so that the two end elastics are on top of each other. Using the knot from above, pull one last elastic through both ends and knot firmly. (This will create a little loop at the end.)

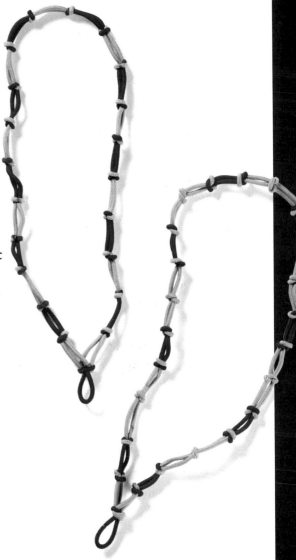

Ribbon-Wrapper Headband

You'll need:
- plain headband that is at least 1 inch wide
- double-sided tape
- 1 roll fabric ribbon
- scissors
- craft or fabric glue

Instructions:
1. Line the top of the headband with double-sided tape.
2. Leaving a long tail (at least 8 inches), wrap the ribbon tightly around the headband, overlapping as you go. Wrap the entire headband.
3. At the end, make another tail of ribbon the same length as the first tail.
4. Apply a small amount of glue around the bottom of each side and wrap the ribbon around one more time to hold it in place. Let dry.
5. Wear as you would a regular headband, but tie the ends to make a bow at the back of the neck.

Tell us why **you** love to dance!

Send your letters to:
Dance! Editor
American Girl
8400 Fairway Place
Middleton, WI 53562

(All comments and suggestions received by American Girl may be used without compensation or acknowledgment. Sorry—photos can't be returned.)

Here are some other American Girl books you might like:

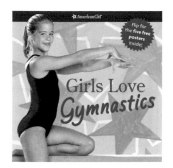

❑ I read it.

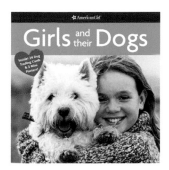

❑ I read it.

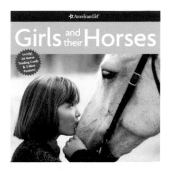

❑ I read it.

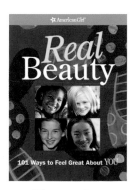

❑ I read it.

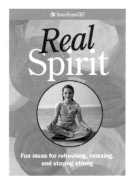

❑ I read it.

❑ I read it.

Dance Posters

Celebrate dance with these tear-out mini posters. Hang them in your room or in your locker, and share with your dance-class friends!

Just dance!

✪ American Girl®

©/™ 2008, American Girl, LLC

★ American Girl®

Dancers
have class!

A dancer lives here.

Do not disturb.
Practice in
progress.